Pieces of My Heart

Wesley Anderson

This book is a work of poetry. Unless otherwise noted, the author and the publisher make no explicit guarantees as to the accuracy of the information contained in this book and in some cases; names of people places have been altered to protect their privacy.

© 2011 First Print © 2013 Second Print
For Wesley Anderson & Published By Maximize Publishing Inc. Bronx New York, All Rights Reserved.

No part of this book may be reproduced, stored in a retrieval system, or transmitted by any means without the written permission of the author.

First Published for: Wesley Anderson & Maximize Publishing Inc.

ISBN-13:
978-0615796420
(Maximize Publishing Inc.)

ISBN-10:
0615796427

Pieces of My Heart

Wesley Anderson

Contents

Foreword

Michael McCain

I want to first say I am honored and privileged by God to have the opportunity to introduce Wesley Anderson to the world as not just a writer, but a poet and an author. Over the course of a few years I have had the privilege of getting to know Mr. Anderson and always knew this day would come. I always found him to be passionate about his work. Making changes and striding to make a mark of excellence always seem to be his goal. When I learned about his book I could not help but offer him my best advice never thinking one day I would be the publisher.

I have read this book cover to cover and portions of it I can relate to and even the ones where I couldn't Mr. Anderson wrote so well it put me in his shoes and made me feel as if I had experienced those same things myself. When I was reading it I chuckled a bit saying; "this is a newborn author". As you read pieces of my heart I am sure you will see small glimpses of Mr. Anderson heart, life and even the future of where his work will take him. I celebrate and congratulate Mr. Anderson for this accomplishment. Now sit back, get a glass of your favorite drink and enjoy the read.

Part I

Acceptance

Forever I tried to solve an unsolvable puzzle

I put all the pieces together

Every aspect fit, except the place where my heart went

Perfection wasn't meant to be mine

But acceptance took it place

Where words were meant to live, silence took its place

Lack of communication means lack of conversation

In the world of understanding, conversations mean everything

I used the key to open up a door that was meant to remain locked

So many times that door slammed in my face

Maybe case in point, why tears never came down my face

Anger and vengeance, both belong to God

The struggle, the sacrifice, the pain, the shame

None of this means anything at all

Through extensive negotiations, we still have no solution

It's like talking to a brick wall

Guards way high, like its day one all over again

Even after years, some things are still unknown

An eternity of emotionally abusive behavior

Though physically available

You're still mentally detached

Though water is still, your ignorance causes surface tension

Pride and wrath make quite a lovely pair

And though love is said

There is only discord here instead

Simple times and loving moments, turned awkward

Alone at night, clinching the sheets for some type of comfort,

As the hole in my heart still remains

Even though I am determined, I can't move stars from the sky

Breaking and taking of mine

In the end, my life is mine

Pieces Of My Heart: Wesley Anderson

In the end of all the madness you make a choice

If you love someone you prove it with actions and follow through with words

Not childish fables

All the blindfolds your heart put over your eyes, removed

All the times you were supposed to prove your worth

You did what only benefitted you

You did what was best for you

I'm like a bird; I'll fly away until I'm happy

I'm like a hornet, I might be small, but at the right time I am strong

At the end of the day, I will never fake what I feel

I won't hold back emotions

I can't be different; I can't be anything less than real

So curse me out, scorn me, and judge me

I believe what I do, if you feel how I feel

Stand up and be nothing less than real

Pieces of me:

I open my eyes to see everything in shambles

I close my eyes and pray when I open them I'll have happiness

Until the day I get it all right, I maintain and hold my ground

We all have demons and my demon is in front of me

Worst part the enemy is a part of me

Worse than that, he is me

Uncontrolled emotions, love aches, and undying devotion

If it were up to me, I wouldn't be so fragile or weak

So here I am, a man that is a lover

Can't change it because I was born that way

Resurfaced

Words were never an option

They kept me wide awake

So I'm lucky to be alive

When no one listened

My words became power

Suicidal intent became poetic energy I spent

When others can't see how I feel, the emotions living on the page are seemingly real

Unlike time, my words can stay in moments and never lose meaning

Love is all that is me

It's my source, the reason, and the motivating factor

Resurfacing is about love and memories

Joy and pain

My struggle and aim

How I check out of reality as Alice's adventures in Wonderland

When I step back nothing is the same

Deprivation

I once was told I was a tiger

Quick and cunning

Strong and fearless

Uncertain I was, to this day I still am

I hate society

I hate social groups, authority, and prejudice

The public is far from intelligent

The masses hold in esteem petty, unreasonable, irrelevant things

Fame is the source of life

Money moves the world

Beauty makes up morals

Sex is a deal breaker

I detest all these things, that's the definition of envy

Trying to do everything by the book

Be humble, kill enemies with kindness

Stand there and smile, think before you react

Give your entire worth; stay stranded only to come out broke

 Life is so bullshit, the government rules

The media breaks reality, to only display false perceptions of the way life should be

I get on my knees and pray

With every bad situation my religion fades away

Time progresses and laps around me before I have time to catch up

Outpaced, it's too late to make a move

As a child I saw a world full of color

Every day I try to see those same colors, all I can make out is grey

Efforts prove futile

Being a human being in this age takes the human away

All that is left is just a being

Pieces Of My Heart: Wesley Anderson

An object, an item, a tool

Despite it all I only work harder

The harder I worked the little I gained

Out of nowhere I was told I can't work so much

Banned from working hard, I suffered hard

Brainwashed by school and told a person with no major is as good as fool's gold

No matter how hard I rehearse I just can't catch the beat or memorize my verse

The mirror ridicules me

The scars of a past not so far

What devastation

In a fit of rage I grew rapidly unhappy

My rapid growth was halted

Like a long jumper, I ran, hit the hurdle and faulted

I was once told I was a tiger

Fangs and claws so strong, I marked my flesh

Fearless enough to not fear death as I tried to sleep myself to health

I became and hence engraved my name on my veins

Others mocked me, laughed at me

Discouraged me, used me, played me

Yet here I am

Purposeless like a thrift store puppet

I feel like I'm a hornet

Tiny and small, but fearless is a hornet

Not just strong, but beyond deadly

Wings to soar beyond limitation

Teeth strong enough to bite the system right back

A stinger to inflict the pain I always felt

A stinger to give back everything I was dealt

My eyes are expressionless as they come

A vacant kind of stare, like a spirit isn't there

The thing I'm searching for is greater than sustenance

The thing I'm hunting down is purpose and there's no way it's escaping me

If not found I'll suffer this accursed disease knows as deprivation

Reinvention

I need the entire world to listen, this is the reinvention

It's time to release and let go

The past, everything about it I don't want anything to remain

I need everyone to forget the old me and realize the person before them is not one in the same

Anger and folly is in the distance

I see the presence of a presence, an apparition of everything former

Growing fast is the thing of yesterday

Being anti-social, I'll save that for another day

Uncertainty, now that's a gift I want to give to another

The pain of self-infliction that's done, I atone

Being a lazy spirit that's preposterous, the soul of a hard worker, now that's an ideal look

Cocky, confident, and cautious, qualities that will be incorporated

Pain use to be my name, but as I allow tears to fall down the sky, symbolic to an emotional cry

I question everything and why I even try

My life is worth less than a bag of chips according to society

Those bastards, those crooks, liars, cheaters, thieves, that's what they believe

I vow

I vow harder than a happily married man, the system's fate I will defy

Dying with a life of emptiness

Dying faithfully unhappy

A person can't accept that

A real human can't respect that, a life characterized by others

Reinvention doesn't happen very fast

It's a possibility it will never last

To be better no matter the cost

I empty my coin purse and prepare to hit them where it hurts

To get a chance to do what I choose

The world can bluff me, but I will never lose

Offbeat

I'm off beat in my way

I could care less what onlookers have to say

I'm looking for love in all the wrong places

All the time, I see smiling faces

I'm trying to be me, trying to live a good life

But I'm stuck trying to find someone to love me right

I'm looking for a lover who can love me right

Hold me tight all through the night

Looking for love in all the wrong places

And all I see is smiling faces

I'm off beat in my own way, but I'm trying to find
somebody who can match what I'm trying to say

An unrhythmic heart trying to catch on to a beat

I'm offbeat looking for a sequence of rhymes

Enough is enough it'll straighten up in time

My heart is offbeat and I know it's just not mine

Music

Music saved my life but I don't owe her anything

Beats and melodies spinning in my head

Songs trapped in my head

While she spread eagle giving it up to everyone instead

Seduced by treble

The day I feel in love, I became a rebel

I climaxed to the pounding of bass

She introduced me to high, highs

Surrounded by sounds

Pieces Of My Heart: Wesley Anderson

The right medium, everything was balanced

She brought out more than audio or visual thoughts, she extracted my talent

When I was feeling down she picked me back up

When anger is on my mind, she provokes me to pick up rage

When I was feeling naughty, the idea of sexy, she seduces me and turns me on

Lights out, nights out, the sun went to sleep on the both of us

When drowned out sound was all that was found, you beamed a flood light, and inspiration was found

Music saved my life, but I don't owe her anything

I put life into her body and made words come to life

I defined a genre that is underwritten

Music use to belong to me, but I only have her when the

beat comes from me

Letters forming words

Thus, words made up a song

No matter how short or long every verse is me and it's still

going strong

Solar powered no need for energy

All you have to do is listen and feel the part of me you are

missing

Fireworks

Night sky

Warm air

A year ago, you were there

Fast forward, just me

It feels surreal to do me

Bright lights, bright smile, it's exactly how it's supposed to be

My fuse is lit; I sense fire coming any day now

A few months ago, I never know a spark was there

My life in the present, nothing else matters

The future is way ahead

In the meantime, I'm going to celebrate the fact every day I should celebrate

A shot of liquor

A socialite with no worries

I'm lost in amazement

I'm like a deer held within the head lights

Bright, warm

Hate and love

Who would have thought ordinary paper could mask explosive

Masking the intent and hunger of the element that causes heat

Soaring into the air at the speed of light

Explosions so vivid it can be seen from space

Pieces Of My Heart: Wesley Anderson

Gigantic shapes covering everything in the background

The life expectancy lasting no less than a second

The fragments fall at what seems to be years

In the glow, my dreams could never be clearer

The need for my cause couldn't be any more in my face

The thoughts and feelings that fled and cause my indifference find their way back

Mind all made up, I'm ready to blow

Every fragment of me will be how it's supposed to be

Sky rocket, hot topic

All the drama, just stop it

My demeanor is much fluid, my outlook much clearer

My will sets a blaze to the night sky

I'm a roman candle, my label says caution

You can't handle me, just leave me where I stand

All debts paid, all restraints dead

Non-believers can keep the negativity

They can have the perks, the end results fireworks!

Aspirations

I want everything positive in this world

I want the love and fame

Love me and adore me

Welcome me into your dwelling; I'll be a household name

I desire the respect from knowing my name

Love is love and I deserve to be king

All is fair when we all do our own thing

When I walk the streets, I want to hear a thousand screams

I want education, wisdom, and success

Give me the task of discovering the impossible

Let me tutor the best, then allow me to school the rest

I want to be wise and scholar-like

With knowledge comes success

No matter the hardship, I'll be known as the dude that's the best

Qualified and held in esteem

Presidential, yet humble

The executive man

Lucrative, luxurious, liable

 Material days, I want them to stay

Glamour and wealth

I want to be included into their threesome

The best relationship ever

To hell with the emotions, I want the financial gain

Every bank will owe me

Every bank will drop stacks just to show me

When the homeless are around, I will toss them far above the poverty line

They shall be a boss and every day they shall floss

Money is like honey

Sweet as hell, yet guarded by the solider bee

Call all the priests, theologist, and monks

Call into existence spiritual properties

Power to heal, power to seal

Starting my footsteps into the kingdom of glory

I want the spiritual ability to give to hope to all

Rewrite the wrongs others have done

No matter what I want to say you'll never be alone

I want to be that dude that has it all

I want glory from every direction

And I want to keep it up like a halo above my head

We all have wants, I have mine

It all may not come to pass, they are just aspirations

Accessory

Idealism and adoration in my head

My hands are idle; guess that makes them a workshop?

I stumbled and I fell off a mountain side

I closed my eyes to escape reality

I'm left with scars, all of my cognitions severed like my nerves

Cut off from my dreams, my heart is at a loss

Like a free style, my thoughts come up lyrically sound

Flowing and going

I'm piecing everything together

I'm rewriting my future, the way I see fit

A lifetime without losers and empty emotions

There is so much apathy in response to the present

With each passing day, I make myself more inanimate

I kill my emotions

In an effort to hold onto my sanity

Everyday I'm doing better now

No more pain, which is no longer my name

I will not answer to that

You, not you that is you, but the you collectively known as us

I separate myself; I can't fight for a cause I don't believe

The air is getting thin, it's no longer easy breathe

I got off the low road for low lives; I'm taking the high road

The road to another chance, another opportunity

The air there is much cleaner

You can no longer put me on

To use to, discarded when no longer necessary

I can only be me, it's not relevant now, but I will be
something almost legendary

For the time being know this to be true:

You can no longer reach me

I am very necessary to my own happiness

Please note, I am no longer an accessory

Flash Flood

Radio silent

I tried to sound the alarm

Nothing came out as the storm approaches

Maelstrom of resentment

I'm up to my knees in defeat; there is no furniture, no bed,
and no sleep

Somewhere in the flood I lost who I was

Pieces Of My Heart: Wesley Anderson

My ship named Stability, washed away

Thunder shakes hopeful days

A tidal wave of emotions sweep me away

Like grains of sand, endless options of what I could do

I'm caught in the undertow of doubt

My current relationship just isn't doing it anymore

I can't fight the current anymore

Nine inches in front of me, I can't even see, it's much too murky

I'm drowning beneath the surface

Consciousness is fading

In the night time sky, the silver lining is waiting

However, not a single trace of the previous state

Thunderstorms and flash floods

Hurricane grade winds, destroyed my drought stricken state

Left in the wake, surviving the storm was just the first part

Being thrown over a thousand miles thanks to a twister

Not knowing which direction to go

All I see are debris from a not so far past

And the sun shines on my back

The first sign of relief and glory

First, I'm able to share this story

Second, with birth must come destruction

Without tragedy, hope has no purpose

Without pain, growth is worthless

So here in a natural disaster's wake, I collect the wood and scattered remains

I have to rebuild my former life, but in a way where only what is necessary fit

All the material things and horded objects, devoured by a higher power

Now day to day is a reward in its self

2 Pieces of glass

Pain is my being because in life I lost my ability to gain

I thrive and survive on being bad because the heart of the matter is I'm mad

I went beyond the point of sadness

I broke free from the chain of madness

It's more like a personal choice

Instead of choosing to be feeble

I got my tiger stripes the hard way--with each incision of the cutter

I held it together, no flinching, I'm fearless, did I stutter?

Not caught up on happy endings, I'm living to die

As far as a broken heart goes, take that and kiss your feelings goodbye

Part II

Loco

Here it goes

Here it flows

Like a drug addict fleeing this plant

Gaining refuge on mars

Sweet nothings whispered and rumors heard from stars

Cosmic breathes from a mental state that comes from being high

Fantasy is far greater than the realities that be

I remember back not long ago

My heart was broken, my morals shattered

Jet setting was my only motive

A void in my soul I tried to fill

Every night was party night

All my pain and shame, it became me

Pieces Of My Heart: Wesley Anderson

It became more than me, it became a religion

I loved the danger

I fell in love with drug induced frenzies

The only problem was there was no love

Following shadows in broad daylight, with no shade in sight

My past life was filled with a lie of a relationship

Attempts of a whore trying to play lover

Wails of jealousy

Hands of greed and vanity

I can't lie; I wanted to be what abused me

With every beat of my heart, I wanted to fall into a rabbit hole

Have the madness of a hatter, I just wanted to matter

Life of the party, I ended up sleeping with Venus

The next day I woke up on mercury

Out of control, I guess, I suppose

Never a dull moment

It seems I was a run on sentence

As my sanity erupts from head

I just want to be bad instead

So here I go, I invite you to a tragedy in my life

A life of beautiful thunderstorms, no smooth sailing, just turbulence instead

Love is not a focal point

At this point I just want what I want

Mind of an antisocial

Its civil unrest

I feel it in my chest

Nothing to follow

I'm walking a dangerous line with no sight

I try to scream or yell

However my jaws broken

I try to take a deep breath, take time to exhale

My throat is crushed

II banged my head on the atmosphere

Pieces Of My Heart: Wesley Anderson

As my cognition suffered a lapse

Depression comes around doing millions of laps

Everybody is so curious to know why the hurt I have is so serious

"It wasn't worth it", they say

"It is just the price to pay; there is no love without hardships"

So I guess I'm supposed to turn my back and say have a great day

It is by far hard to cope with the excruciation

All I have is my psychological tattoo

My eyes project the inception of fear

I tremble when my memories are too close

I just lay on the ground

Defenseless, I surrender my power

Heartless, I stare at you

I'm a lover not a fighter, so I've been told

Now I'm feeding off the pain

I am not content in the condition I'm in

My heart made me stay, yet love drove me away

Pieces Of My Heart: Wesley Anderson

Mentally fatigued, broken down to the size of a eukaryote

Is life purgatory and this situation inner hell?

I rock back and forward as if I'm a ghost in a shell

Shrieking and deranged, I'm mad

In the asylum, distorting the fabric of time

In my mind, I'm just an antisocial

In my mind, there is only one answer to every solution

Critical of everything around

Ruled by the pain, yet I still remain

Uneasy, as the wind brushes against my skin

Angel, fallen out of grace at best

Nearly obtaining this dream, only to be erased from the scene

Exhausted from the overwhelming pressure

Take out the double edge sword!

Like Excalibur driven into my heart

Inscribe in Rosetta, that I wish not to be stoned

I want to create a better version of the person known as me

I just want to do it alone

Child

Burn after burn

I'm discouraged

I'm a child in the shell of a man

I'm embarrassed; I don't know what to say

My indifference holds me

As a result focus hasn't had a chance to mold me

Like others my age

I feel like I'm defective

Right now my heart is broken

I'm regretful, I feel like an outsider amongst my family tree

This place where I belong,

I need to find it quick

Close my eyes and I know without a doubt this is where I belong

Close my eyes and know it's my home

Pieces Of My Heart: Wesley Anderson

To be honest, I don't feel human

My psychotic episodes and collection of memories
reinforce the fact

Reinforce the fact, I feel I lack

I lack what others do

The emotions and raw potential

I want to feel confident

I want to know one day I can be influential

I'm lying here, staring here

I depended too much on others to move me

As a child, which I still am

I had a phobia of places with a mass of people

I never felt one with everyone

Always disconnected, I feel like an alien here

I drive for miles hoping to stumble onto my purpose

Accelerating to an invisible goal

Decades ago, I thought love would set me free

I searched and I thought if I gave my all it would be given
back to me

Pieces Of My Heart: Wesley Anderson

Here, begins the story of tragedy

Maybe it was all circumstance

Maybe, it would be different somewhere else

Maybe I wouldn't hurt myself, because of what others say

Maybe a life of faith would be my mainstay

If my mind could be projected it would be all grey

Grey skies, rain all day

Grey lands, damp and moist

Grey water, pushing everything away

Emotions and opinions all hijacked from me

I'm alone and afraid to be only me

I don't even know me

I yell

I Scream

Punch a hole in the whole room

No answer comes

Only silence

I pray to get understanding

But part of me doesn't believe

Part of me hasn't grasp the jest of life itself

Not thinking in abstractions

No logic so I predict that as evil

So in turn, that evil is a part of me

So in turn, I hate that part that manifests and consumes me

I hate the blank look and the emptiness of responses

I hate the images of a box cutter on the floor

Myself in the bath tub, knee deep in red water

Wounds deeper than anything I've ever seen

Free flowing like a mighty river

Flowing out to escape me

The scene still haunts me

How can I glance at myself and just say I'm ok?

How can you just wish it all away?

I'm this child stuck in this shell

It offers no protection to this hell

I'm a child who knows nothing at all

Full of embarrassment, loss of self

Loss of help

Curled up in a fetal position, because I'm weaker than a fetus

No hopes or dreams

I lost all that when I abandoned myself for other people

I gained the anger to endure deaths touch

Instead of dying, it's like a public execution every single day

It's like losing your religion and not knowing your way

I have fallen away

All I want to do is have a purpose

All I want to do is matter and have value

All the wishes in the world can't make this happen:

Grow up from being a child

Be a man in my own right

Muscle, might, or strength can't subdue the sheer power of him

Logic, wisdom, or words do justice by him

Full of glory, you can see light in his face

Brave, powerful, resourceful, proof within his eyes

Love, peace, and prosperity filled in every touch he uses

No words have to be said, respect follows his every move

Here I am in a child's place

How do I become better and over step my limits?

Resignation

Why was I never enough?

I poured my heart out, you threw me away

Replaced, again by yet another

Maybe the placement of me was never meant to be

I wanted to die, suicide to fill my empty void

All I wanted was to matter, in this position I'm nothing

I loved hard, I just wanted the same

I guess I wasn't sexy enough

I can't compete with the other individuals

My heart is a sheet of ice, your body, burning like a wildfire

I guess I wasn't exciting enough

Pieces Of My Heart: Wesley Anderson

Holding hands, watching the rain, simple things were wanted

Electronegative, you took my spark

I guess strong enough I was not

I formally say I'm sorry

All the times I made you mad for just being me

All the times I slept by myself

My words only got me sent away

Just another person, dime a dozen

I guess well enough I am not

When I became dull, you flirted with other people

Straight face on, all I heard were lies

You didn't run behind me or care that I cried

It didn't stop me from getting my questions answered

So I stopped asking question

With my final tears, I cry, make pathos derail

Emotions in my mouth, stale

In the stale-mate of fighting for love, I give up and just let the love once held die

Here it goes, from this day, end of our road

I decided to travel my life alone

Resignation from a futile type of commitment

Mark my words, this it I quit

Criminal

Line me up

Conduct a body cavity search

Accuse me of every crime in the world

Handcuff me to a stop sign

Match my fingerprints to the scene of the crime

Caught red handed, I'll be red herring

The verdict taken from God's hands, all seeing eyes
replaced by that of men

The person of interest, suspect, culprit, everything in
reference to a wanted man

No longer human, state property

Pieces Of My Heart: Wesley Anderson

No longer human, just damaged goods

All the evidence makes me look like the trigger man

My footprints in every direction, although physically I was never there

Guilty before I got a chance to plead my case

All my vision distorted, blinded by mace, the media says I resisted arrest

Held in contempt for how my time was spent

Persecuted by a hung jury

The death penalty they say to me

I'll meet everyone there at the electric chair

Charged with every crime in the book

Charged for being nothing more than me

The world knows me more than I could ever identify me

Detained and charges pressed, without warrants for my arrest

If I have to go away for a remembrance of me to stay

Pull the lever, no pun intended and nothing more or anything clever

High voltage and sparks implode

Cutting the power as I sit there, lifeless, strapped to the chair

Social death, by the power of others

Adverse effects

I feel it in the wind

I feel it in my skin

Others can't see it

Others don't know it

But, it hastily approaches

There is no running

There is no escaping

The inevitable is forthcoming

You smile at me

You say it's ok

But, ok will come around another day

Pieces Of My Heart: Wesley Anderson

I'm holding on the edge of my seat

You approach me, but you have no idea

You have no clue about what it takes

To qualify for the position that needs to be filled

In time you will see my rapid development

In time you will see my constant intelligence

My build will seem so unreal to you:

There it is, all on deck

No bitterness attached to these bittersweet memories

Everything's all sweet on my end

I'm over the situation, but it seems circumstance isn't quite over me,

I smile at the fact you were hurt

I'm satisfied in the few months you replaced me

I could care less about the hole in your heart

I'm unconcerned about your day to day struggle

Everything was on the line and all you had to do was give me a peace of mind

Nothing you can say will change how real it's going to get

I'm tired of listening to lies

I'm tired of being led on, only to be stranded in the end

You see me as a crutch and not this amazing man

You only want me for my help, when I can help you so many ways

I gave up on you the instant you said "walk out of my life"

You can keep that broken heart

You can hold onto everything you gave me

All that is inside of you is hatred

Other people see you as a fool

You really make people want to give up hope

Unable to make it because, you haven't grown up yet

Still a child, still a weak kid

Dependent on others, not an ounce of independence

Leaning on others, never looking to yourself

Mirror

So quick to hold on close

To walk away from the truth, is the journey of a fool

Questioning my own motives

Second guessing when I should say what I know

Hurt because I can't say exactly what I feel

Love blinds us and distorts what is real

Perception becomes reality, while the latter is a fantasy

I see the face of my people; you are so similar to me

We are at the same place, but in different directions

Opposing emotions, reflecting what the other has to say

As long as I can see you I know the light of truth exists

When shadows from deception lurks, I know the mirror won't work

Clouded in darkness the truth comes out missing

We are the same type of person, only in opposite directions

Trying really hard, gazing in the mirror I'm trying to see the person you are

I want to understand

Friends

I redefined the lines

I've experienced a ton

I have knowledge of an elder although I'm still young

I'm frowned upon for my seemingly illogical actions

Bound by meaningless words

Friend, in the end that cursed word I wish to disown

A heartless stray clinging unto your coat tail

Resentful cunt, whose means is to corrupt my flow

I came across many and I've searched within for the detestable meaning of this word friend

Mysterious like a shadow with no source

I try to abide by the rules and let nature take its course

Pieces Of My Heart: Wesley Anderson

I scream at the top of my lungs

Rock bottom is hit, falseness has built up

A tower of lies and crushed dreams

Haunted by confused expectations

Here I've witness death of many innocents

Executed as a display at the stakes

Broken down, dragged to the ground

Sacrificed wellbeing for another's sake

My mistake is that I'm too harsh, I'm too fake

Says the person I suppose was my friend

The feeling of reaching my goals foiled

Used only for selfish goals

I've been the victim of this crime

Locked in a world of pain

These friends are guilty of the following

Bleeding my veins dry

Crushing my bones

Temptation from them so formidable

While I am so weak

Pieces Of My Heart: Wesley Anderson

Sleepwalking without sleep

Tossed aside like an old girls doll

Forgotten by her ambition to be with boys

I'm a boy, a boy that's unwanted

Undesired, damaged goods

Rancid milk, disposed

Rumors of fire, lies sure do spread

My vengeance burring like a Nazi furnace

My morals shell shocked like a veteran soldier

Begging for bread, yearning for nourishment

The old me is now homeless

Walking this cold world solo

Alone I am strong

Not able to wrap my mind in the gravity of it all

Yet I stand tall

I could never transcribe the forbidden transitions others
have tried to instill in the outer reaches of my head

You cannot chisel into a heart of stone

Watching that accursed word torture life like hazardous waste

Butchering nonsense until it was made logical

Friends can be cold murderous inglorious bastard

To be more specific this friendship thing is through

Caught in a civil war

I run by myself

Successfully evading landmines of deception

Where I'm trying to go is my destination

You may say I'm stupid

You may say I'm shrewd

So let bygones be bygones

And allow me to force myself to be strong

Abandoned

Time has slowed down

The moon doesn't shine

On the opposite horizon the sun just sits there, black and no longer full of life

I look around and it's just me there

Each foot step in the darkness is as painful as the last

Clenching my heart to subdue the pain

In this life there are no words, only actions

With my eyes closed, I try to imagine earth

The bright blue sky, the interactions and bonds I valued

Also the existence of lies, misuse, and abuse

Constant agony and trying to maintain

Constant put downs

Most of all living with the fact: multitudes hate me

Not intense dislikes, just down right hate me

Going with the flow, I turn on myself and I hate me too

Pieces Of My Heart: Wesley Anderson

Losing all my strength at once

I question my own existence

And I doubt the truth, because what has the truth done besides hurt me?

On planet earth the wind blows

On the planet that is our home, the winds flows and goes where it pleases

Just like rumors and diseases

No longer gentle, it breaks through any stronghold

It cuts through steel and twist it like tin foil

So what chance do I have?

This other dimension, doomed with eternal rain

In this realm every second is like reopening every wound

I kill my emotions and throw away hope to become another person

Someone who will never get hurt

Love, relationships

Hope, dreams

Faith, devotion unreal

All separate from me

In reality with it all gone, I'm not much like me at all

And that's ok

It's ok to never cry again

It's ok to never feel misunderstood

In the still of darkness is only me

Everything I wanted does not exist here

Maybe in the world of light it never existed either

So I'm torn, because nothingness is what I wanted

Nothingness is all I've got

Its pain

It hurts

Truth is no one can imagine the degree in which I hurt

Combined blood, sweat, and tears

With my mind, body, and soul

All I was left with, exhausted effort

Now I'm here

In this place that doesn't make sense

Where I'm as alone as I feel

Got lost in the search, looking for love

Now surviving in this realm

This reality known as hell

Detached from the things that make me, me

I hate myself, because I hate ever misunderstood part of me

I hate the loneliness and abandoned me

Black out the sun and let the mighty rain fall

Now I live exactly how I feel

So take all my feelings of love, trust, and hope

Abandon me again, but please this time makes it for real

Rainfall

It's raining where I am

I don't know where you are

It's storming outside

I have my pullover on

In the waters of the sky, I well cleanse the weakness

Pieces Of My Heart: Wesley Anderson

Ask the wind, ask the stillness of night

Search for an answer and I'll hold on to it

My immunity is low, but through a maelstrom, I must go

No light shed upon it

No finger prints upon it

No pointing the finger at me and say I done it

Flashlight in hand

Aiming at the road

What's behind me will remain such

I have to get where I have to go

No rushing on this road though

Simple words and a heart full if valor will make the way

Even if the ditches overflow, my feet might get somewhat wet

No trench foot, I've gotten out of the ravine

Thunder flashes to discourage my traverse

Lighting threatens the journey I've made so far

Each drop of rain throws all of its might to slow me down

The mud holds my feet

From solid concrete to mud and clay

I'm on my way to discover something new

Things that only the forgotten may know

No sunshine in sight, here the storm is perpetual

Sirens scream, singing songs of ruin and lust

Going on my way I pass them with nothing to say

My pullover well drenched

Caught in the mighty fall

Wind and water forge into one

A ghastly combination they have become

Here I go trying to make things happen

I have always heard when it rains it pours

Frostbite

The ice starts to fall, and I can feel the cliff begin to unravel

From underneath my feet, the waters and wind start to come marching in

Like a hurricane

Pieces Of My Heart: Wesley Anderson

The dust as well as dirt starts to reveal all the signs of hurt and pain

In the form of a blizzard

Treading on thin ice

Thin sheets of memories that use to complete it

The lake once called the heart

Once a sub-tropical climate

Turned arctic thanks to global warming

The lack of focus, the fussing, that was the first warning

All alone on this island of ice

It's all mental, no escape in sight

My mind has been damaged

Although we both share this bed

It feels like the other is just dead

We occupy the space, no conversation to be made

In a bed so tiny, it seems we come from different galaxies

Living with you is getting so old, way too cold

I'm in need of heat

Pieces Of My Heart: Wesley Anderson

Beyond the white, the only thing I see is the red covered snow

Fingertips punctured again

With every passing day no middle ground

My lows so low I can't make a sentence

My highs, heart stopping and ominous

Nose bleeds from the altitude

The table I sit at every day is on the state border

Roman numeral number one, a state requiring the faith and strength that only god can give

Roman numeral two, a state making pain seem eternal

Every passing hour reminds me of Antarctica

Sugar brought me here

Stripping me of vision slowly

Robbing the lengths of my days

Permafrost hugs the answer I have been searching for

An all day and night winter land

Brought to you by diabetes

The junction of me and you

I want you to cheat and find another

Perhaps give me a few minutes out of the day to regain my composer

Give me a moment where without a jack I can breath

A moment where blood does not come out bright red

Standing at amongst the snow

Frost bitten yields amputation

No balance or heat around

A day in a world full of snow is a world trying to make it out the snow

However the sun is present here, so there must be a way

Insulin is the coat and at the present moment I need it the most

Snake bite

It's coursing through me

The fluid moves through my veins

I shake and tremble

My body goes blank, and my mind goes numb

Everything is confusing

I want to speak, but my saliva escapes me

All I have is this cotton mouth

Everything becomes bright

I was at this place

Where I have both lost and won

I was abandoned by my first love

Where I stand is where I gained another's heart

In this spot, a lot took place

The place where I left my heart and found it next to a ring that was lost

Waters from the river wash away the pain, yet the tide brings in memories

There is no such thing as seasons here

Love and hate mingle

Every contradiction coexists happily

Now I stand here in a somewhat altered present

Different from the future I thought of then

Pieces Of My Heart: Wesley Anderson

I didn't think I would lose this much

I never thought I'd be the one

I never thought I'd be the one saying never

It's like the ground crumbled beneath me, I come to another dimension

All I can make out is hissing

Scales rub me the wrong way

More like mocking and less like rubbing

The liquid begins to spread fast

I can see auras now

I'm full of regrets that color translates to blue

I'm trying to figure out how to be a better man

Once on the brink of death, love kept me from flat lining

Taking me on one hell of a roller coaster ride

There is nothing personal to feel, I just have to allow reality to take over

My love like wings on my back and the name of my lover sewn to my soul

I'm starring off into space hands to my chest

See the truth is, I've been bitten by a serpent

I was reflecting on the reflection from the water of the past

And this snake just so happen to past by

Held my hand out to reach out to a former me, but the snake bite an unaware me

Now the poison courses through my body

The fluid has stunned me in a way I cannot say

It's do or die now

It's either give up or just stand up

Anti-Venom

The shadows begin to fade

It's a minute before a minute and I see a million lights

The main color I see is red

The brightness of passion, yet the representation of mad

Paralysis takes me over

I'm holding on, but in desperation of a remedy

I try to form a complete thought, but logic is lost

Pieces Of My Heart: Wesley Anderson

And I feel is water in my head

My ears are flooded by half truths

And most of all my heart misses you

Most of all my body is super confused

I'm dehydrated, yet I'm wet all over

Disconnected

There's a tingling sensation, followed by a slow burn

Maybe I was foolish and I have a lot to learn

I'm ready if you're ready

Get inside of me; please do what you are supposed to

My survival depends on you

Even though I couldn't see it, there's some missing normality

I'm flat on my back but I'm flying

Feels like I'm speeding by

I clear everything away, the thoughts and emotions

Try to form a clean slate

The doctors stand over me and yell clear

I fibrillated when I thought I was only meditating

The anti-venom couldn't hurt any better

I struggle for strength with each passing hour

And when I wake up its raining and I'm standing in an afternoon shower

Amnesia is the reason, but this place seems familiar

The past and the future seems so far away

I don't quite understand

I think I had everything figured out

However, the thoughts reasons and logic escape my head

I'm forgetting a major part of why I came here

Everything began with an encounter from a snake

I just sit here and stare wondering if in my instincts I possess what it take

Part III

Chain smoke

I open the pack up

There is only one intention

Cloud everything by smoke

Others call it abuse of a substance

True smokers call it a chain

My soul falls to the ground

My body is lazy

A crowd full of faces

Mocking and laughing

My head is pounding

My heart seems like it's not even beating

Half dead and half alive in an isolated corner

I feel like a puppet on strings

I feel like the devil has his hands at my feet

Hell's mouth is open and demons are smiling at me

A pack of cigarettes ago I thought it was sexy

One is never enough

With arms wide open I want the tobacco to make love to me

I desire to be slave to the alcohol in my cup

With a sirens voice it tells me to smoke up

Boost my high then touch the sky

Every flick of my Bic burns away a portion of my life away

I swear all I need is another pack

Each cigarette like a struggle present in my life I'm haunted by

I drink an entire bottle then finish another pack

Tears in my eyes as everything goes slow

Wearing a big fat grin, when it comes to being drunk off my ass I don't want to be the person that wins

Blacked out on the floor

Flirty person standing on top of the stage

Half-dressed with vomit pouring out my mouth

Phone calls and texting pouring in

Where did I go?

What did I do?

Guess it's just the dangerous of drinking and smoking a bit too much

I need another pack stat; my party friend won't shut up

I only have a single hour before it's time to get up

One hour to sleep off after effects, put on a fake smile and go back to work

Oh no, I don't want that so much

Being "that" person who lost their purpose in life

Too bad I'm a causal smoker and smoking isn't my thing

A cigarette in the form of a person

Standing there smoking one's self

A person unable to stop and needing extra help

Smoke break is up, no thanks I'll pass

Fair well

You're stealing it away

You got me hungry and wasting away

It's like I'm listening to a sirens song

I glance at you and instantly you intimidate me

When I grow closer to the ladder of greatness,

You kick me off

All the wounds have healed, yet you're ready to cut them open

My head is finally clear, yet you add unneeded confusion

I rest soundly asleep, but you shake me until I am awake

I don't want you close by

I don't want to see you, because in essence I don't want you

You shove hard into my skin

You mark me up with corruption

When I'm at my weakest, you drive me insane

Your presence makes me deranged

Once something I use to love

Now we have love and hate

You love to hurt me

And I hate how you treat me

I'm leaving this abusive relationship

My one true addiction

My desire for pain

I'm no longer at your mercy

And since you're far away, I won't let you hurt me

Farwell to you sinful, painful

Abusive love

Confessions of hopeless romantic

The crushing of hopes in illusions

I have never gotten used to it

Having emotions and expectations

A positive outlook full of sunshine

Pieces Of My Heart: Wesley Anderson

Optimism so bright, it rivals the sun

Yet behind closed doors, the sadness slips from underneath the bed

All the things I have said, all the selfless acts, dead

Sealed shut in a haunted room, my greatest gift is my weakness

A heart made of stainless steel made faulty

Oxidation occurs and produces rust

Surrounded on all sides, yet I am all alone

Misconception is my own fault, I caused this penalty

With all my emotional and spiritual strength, I hold back my tears

No such luck

Back to crying again

Back to feeling misunderstood again

I find myself being left out of the loop again

The mirror holds my reflection, but there is only a blank canvas

Still trying to paint a pretty picture, yet everything is blank instead

Pieces Of My Heart: Wesley Anderson

I try to give and provide for others, yet I'm the one whose will is ending

I channel everything in my head, like a cognitive television

One season after another, the young and the restless, everything repeats again

At the finale, always left at the end

My heart aches are like the dance floor

Everybody in the same world as me moves and grooves to their own beat

Here I am struggling trying to move my feet

No rhythm, no soul, so the only thing left is to flail around

I exit my head and head outside instead

The wind blows here, and I can visualize all the memories

So here it goes

All alone again, this part is called soul searching

Twenty-one years down, how many more to go?

I have to find an idea or concept

There it goes again, separated

I just want there to only be one

I search, even when I don't try to my heart

Searches for the one to make me happy, make me complete

How can I be happy when I'm the enemy to me?

How can I be happy when the problem here is me?

I can't be happy because there is so much I don't understand about me

Just staring off into space, I can picture the everything pour out

I relive every moment of mistrust and failed love, all at once

What more do I have left to give

Nothing more for me to say

I guess the game might just end this way

Wanting to be appreciated

Wanting to be seen as everything I am

These feelings, this darkness it approaches

And when I'm alone I just feel soulless

Majority of the times my words don't matter

It's like I'm a child, with no absolution

I just want to heal

Everything I have given

Everything that was taken

I need at least half back

ugly

All you have to do is just say it

We are at the defining moment

A moment of truth where only truth should matter

Instead of being praised for my character

I'm told my looks are what matter

Setup for display, others don't seem to think I have what it takes

The majority say I'm worthy

Not nothing new or out the ordinary

For others to say I'm ugly

Nothing any different from yesteryear

Someone to testify for me, someone to be my witness

Its people like that are the reason why hate resides in one's self

Constantly judging as if they themselves are worthy

They talk about your shape

They hate the way you were supposed to be made

Every detail god mad flawless, stained by flaws of mankind

Perfection is only within in your head

Perfection, is the imperfection of being called human

Although my age is older each day

My image, never good enough

Everything less than amazing

I would cry, but it seems the well is dry

For over two decades, I tried to rearrange myself

Tried to make my look more appealing to everyone

No matter how much you try or how much effort you've burned

At the end of the day you're still ugly

Fingers pointed at you

Eyes rolled, excuses made on why people can't like you

Personality is good, but you're too damn ugly

Again and again

I roll around the topic as if I'm the one that's foolish and vain

I blame myself when you're the one to blame

Also called insane, when your vision is the vision obscured

As if life were hard enough, my appearance is made like it's the worse

Eyes piercing through my very soul, as if it were transparent

Trying to read into me

Speaking ugly about the things I've done in the past

Constantly breaking me down, then rebuilding with more durable material

Twisting every positive thing I say, ugly ears are always near

I didn't get that was the way life should go

Slandering everything that makes people, people

Robbing me of my credit when my credit is far from due

The laughs, the smiles

Falsehood in every miserable tooth

People say I'm ugly

Taking away all that shines within

People say I'm ugly

Playing the judge when they are also criminal

People say I'm ugly

You know what; I'm perfectly fine with that

People say I'm ugly

That's perfectly fine, don't waste your time

People say I'm ugly

But what exactly is ugly?

Isn't beauty a subjective perception of attraction?

Subjective meaning to each its own

Attraction being what turns you on

I apologize for being the person you don't see fit

Enough of the insecurity shit

What do you get for hiding under a rock, separating from others?

I rather stand there and be stoned for being ugly plus more

Nowhere in the world is there another me

Not a single person in the galaxy who can be anywhere close to me

See it's far from the first time or the last time someone will call me ugly

So ill cling to the truth formerly called ugly

Timeless classic, the next big thing since black

Ugly is what I might be

But my physical being is nothing but an elaborate shell

Fire soul

You though you could get to me

You thought all the pain and hurt would work

I allowed you to reach my soul

From this day the only remnant of us will be fireworks

I have the gas can in hand

For so long you drenched my heart with lies

In the same way I see fit, I'll cover everything in gasoline

You were quick to turn to anger

In retaliation, I'll just set everything on fire

I have the intention in the palm of my hands

Without any effort, I'll will turn a quiet night into an incent filled festival night

It's no need to beg for mercy

No need to cry and plead for your life

If the flames won't reach you, I know you choking on your own false promises will leave you at a loss

Oxygen like you, is not helpful here

A prophet said revenge is a dish best served cold, but I can't wait to serve it up

So I bake it up, seven fold of the original time

In a trance from the pyre

I've scarified so much in this very fire

Except you

Except the source of my anguish

I'll make everything burn black

No light, no feelings or emotions evolved

Pieces Of My Heart: Wesley Anderson

For you to be on the receiving end, I'll do whatever it takes

See you have 10 seconds to understand who runs the show

You have 10 seconds to realize what you have

5 seconds left my back turned, wings mounted on my back

The intent to leave, with no promises to ever return

Let's compare this to desert storm

You use guerilla warfare tactics

And I'll use napalm to flush you out

Your life known as a jungle, incinerated

Charred, no foliage

No hope or trees

Rend asunder in the wake of a fire storm

All smiles on my face, call me an arsonists

Heat coming from my chest, in the inferno I burn my name alas

And I walk away fire soul, controlled by burning rage

Man on fire and man of the flames

Lover's revenge

Plunging into a pool of shallow lies

Listening to your bullshit ass lies

Your precious lips glowing in the sun

But when the moon hits

The script flips, twisting into an ugly art form

Seducing father time himself to do your selfish bidding

Corrupting the innocent

Tainting the purest of hearts

Licking your lips at the sign of bloodshed

Too bloodthirsty you're superhuman

You're a monster in disguise

The filthy thoughts in your head

Condemn all until you get what you want

Using your insensitive claws to crush souls

Foul and fierce

Pieces Of My Heart: Wesley Anderson

You are the prey

I'm your next victim it's clear as day

Simply irresistible, fulfilling all my pleasurable needs

You get on your knees

You do all it takes to please

Yourself, not me

I want your crazy, evil, and shame

I want to be the reason you forget my name

I want to be the one you hate that you're attached to

The person you feel you need too

To be your false lover, boyfriend number three

I want us to pretend to be

I want to use you how you used me

I see through you, but you can't see me

Capture your heart from the start

Get your hopes really high

Then crush them, rush you to the alter and say I do,
knowing I really don't

Pieces Of My Heart: Wesley Anderson

Lay you to pasture and devour you alive, but we both know you're the man-eater

I need your sexy, your gorgeous, and your seduction

Use a hammer and demolish you

Put on a stone cold poker face

I want to bluff you and fold you in high stakes

I want your rhythm, your glory, and fame

I want your choreography, lyrics and steps

Take the beat clean out of your heart

Dirty Diana, that's the person I know you want to be

Take it for granted

Then burry you alive

My eulogy won't contain any apology

Give me your sight, your vision, your mindset

Make you psychotic while being chaotic

Half breed mix, I want your Asian, your Spanish, and French

Create a coupe, so I can misuse you

Lend me your hand, your might and your mainstay

Pieces Of My Heart: Wesley Anderson

I'd promise I'd stay, only to lead you astray

Show me the inner you

I'd curse you, cut you, court you

A fitting punishment for the things you are accustomed to

Give me your lonely and crazy stare

The innocent thoughts in your head

Loan me your identity and security

Break your guard then have you wanting more, dismiss
you like dismiss actions of gold digging

My joy, indifference, and tolerance only remain

Give me all the things that are priceless

Pawn everything away

I'm not your toy and I'm not your friend

I'm not your baby, boyfriend, nor kin

I'm a phantom, a mistake, and empty promise

I'm your heartless, your needy, your sin

I'm a monster, an abomination, a creature

I eat hearts and I collect minds

I'm your reason, the lack gained ground

You're the reason my love is so bleak

I've turned the tables and forced you to eat

Delectable candy, love; my treat

If you think love's really sweet and kind

Sit at the table and taste mine

Revenge in a bowl prepared just for you

Spoon in hand, I give it to you

Time for alone time, just you know me

Pieces of my heart:

So you want a man to call your own?

Better open your eyes and peep game fast

My heart is so big, but time doesn't wait forever

If you want this, better fix your lips to say something

Money isn't a factor; we live one life and can't take it anyway

Words mean nothing to me, how about action

How about we go deeper than sexual attraction?

How about we talk about ownership over leasing?

Not the type to invest in nothing without my love,

I promise it'll be like life is nothing

And if you're willing to progress then true love we can gain

Dream chaser

I'm a dream chaser

Running after a dream like speed racer

I left my brain a thousand miles away

My motivation lies in my demonstration

All that is left, determination

I said I loved you

What I didn't know was that love would cost

I'm a star chaser, trying to keep a fleeting wish

My right brain wants to just turn away

Pieces Of My Heart: Wesley Anderson

My left brain entertains mind games

Soaring on wings of steel

The will of fire

This love lacks passion and logic

If both are missing, what is it I desire?

You are heavy hearted, made of stone

Yet, I want you to fly me past the sky

I am a fantasy chaser; I like to hear tall tales

I enjoyed the story about two estranged lovers

One was dedicated, the same one was jaded

One was constantly faded, everything sentimental was hated

The two where polar opposites, yet they attracted

Like oil to water, it did not quite mix

Hydroplaned they did

One lover was devastated, while the other was apathetic

Deviated from the collision course, separate ways they were sent

I can relate

The reason I became a chaser

Following lyrics with no sound

A heartbeat minus words

I am a love chaser

Following ideas, concepts, theories, and proposals of love

Basing life on chasing love with no end

Just when it looks like it's over, my love I surrender

Close my eyes look for promises of affection and nights so tender

A double edged sword, a gift and curse

My heart cursed with this thing that's a splinter

Atchafalaya Basin Love

Days and nights merge into one

 Blissful kisses rivaled by the sun

Romantic walks with the moon in the background

Flying higher than any space man

Floating in the clouds longer than any weed head

Nothing feels better than laying my head in your bed

The taste of summer time inundating on tongue

All I have to do is cross a simple bridge

Listen to some slow jams, because I know, without a doubt I'm wanted for who I am

It doesn't matter if the fog hides the way

Your heart makes everything transparent

The might of a thunderstorm doesn't scare me

No matter what I'll make it safe to you

In the midst of everything I know I just have to make it to you

Three counties away, I'll walk for hours

Baby, the commitment we own gives me power

Like the bridge there's no lack of connection

Stay with me and I'll be your protection

Crush

I'm astonished

I'm amazed

I'm stuck on you

I would say it's a phase, but I'm addicted to you

Nothing major, Just little things we do

Kissing and holding

Playing around, arguing

Truth is told you; I want to be with you until I grow old

Cherish this love

Find out your main frame

Hack your emotions

Use my technical skills to show you digital love

If our love is ever lost, I'd bring it back at any cost

Sail away on an odyssey

Just to get you back

I can show you where true love is really at

Once I say those three words there's no turning back

If you used me, I won't turn my back

I'd never hurt you or lie behind your back

If you ever need me

I'll always reside, look into my eyes, my heart I won't hide

Promise you'd never leave me lonely

Until time erodes away if you put faith in me I'd never go away

I want to share aspirations, encouragement, and dreams

Turning your darkest night into the clearest day

Here I'll stay, here I say, nothing could make me go away

We all make mistakes I'm willing to endure whatever it takes

I want to be your symbol of love

Part IV

Johnny on the spot

When I heard a love song I thought I would miss you

Without you better I do

Seeing is believing and the way I see everything

You better believe you will see it too

No matter how gigantic the leap or the fall

No matter the consequences

My mind refuses to go back to you

My mind is stationary, but my heart goes to the stars

We probably could have went far

Circumstance after circumstance, everything lacked romance

I love it right here, departed and unaccompanied

The horizon, the fading of light

Everyone can have someone

Everybody can find their definition of love

To me there is way more to it

The object I'm searching for

I have to talk about it, rave about it

Razzle dazzle, sparkle and shine

Beyond everything, I just want to hear, "you are mine"

One on one time is what I want

Affection so true

Solace, communication

The idea of comfort

I want sexy conversations, tangible love making

Discernments so bright, call what we were to own star bright

Sex is not a determining factor, but I will perform like an 18th century actor

I have to add to my success, when it comes to love I will never be nameless

See my actions and thoughts intertwine into one

I want a natural connection from day one

Date after date, I want to be anxious for the next

Pieces Of My Heart: Wesley Anderson

I seek the knowledge of knowing there is more to me than
I can see

Most of all, the fact that another human wants to see

Don't give a bad review if one day I don't see your point of
view

So here I go a hopeless romantic with beats in his head

He rather devise that, than mediocre melodies instead

My heart never beats hopeless

 Even if stones crack every piece of my amity

I will never lie on broken glass

Even in uncompromising positions

My joy is my unyielding position

No matter what I will always occupy this spot

When doubts flood up to my door and I'm head high in a
sea of despair

My love will fight through the pain

Regardless if a lover feels the same

I will not stop until it travels into their brain

My mouths create the words no matter

In the darkest of hours only the actions will matter

No reputation will be necessary

Everything I'm fond of will be taken care of

In the end my love is nothing less than, Johnny on the spot

Heartbeat

I try to find you

I haven't seen you

But when I lay down I'm next to you

Laid down, cuddled up, protecting you

I'm no superman

But you emboss the S on my chest

And when I stare into your deep eyes

I confess my life has been a mess

So much tragedy and drama I remove from my chest

If only I could speak to you

Spend countless hours together

The heavenly sensation when we're next to each other

From the get go, I'm yearning for more

If only me and you would meet

I'd promise to show you how this thing called love goes

I'd do what others won't

I'd do it like a pro

Pin you to the bed, kitchen table, or floor

Reaching to Your inner most core

If only we could meet

I'd show you every day in life was a treat

As long as you were with me you'd see

If only I could see your face

Touch your body

Break it down

No hesitation or sound, no conformation

Only anticipation

As I have the desire with the aim to please

My claim to fame

If only I'd had a chance

I'd prove I could be a man

Give you sentimental things

Kissing in the rain

Playing in the sand

Looking at the river

Heartbeat, you're the one my soul seeks

I reach my peak

Even without you I feel your body heat

Commitment

Put all my eggs in the basket

Slip into a coma

Put my dreams in a casket throw you in the forefront

And I'll lie there until you call out to me

Words can't express how I want to be with you

As you learn more and more you run the risk of losing all you've known

In a single instant the one that doubles your heart

Ends the act, breaks your heart, once again lonely

Pieces Of My Heart: Wesley Anderson

My world upside down, no laughter closeness or sound

I run the risk, but I take my discretion

I can't come on too strong or hunt you down

Can't be too picky, freaky, or needy

Give me your hand, allow me be your man

As I treat you light-years better than a one night stand

Caress your body

Turn off the lights cuddle you tonight

Being with you makes everything feel like a late night, so right

Let me be your prince

Hold it down

Let put my all into the moments shared

Putting my all into these formidable question

How can I make sense if I'm in love?

I'm so damn nervous, I'm terrified

Scared to be in love, ashamed of being hurt

My war torn heart bleeds out with discord

It's like I'm in cardiac arrest and I can't stop swarming

I'm losing myself and it's involuntary at best

If I get hurt I'd tell you this, I'm glad I put up with it all

I've tried my best, not your husband material so on to the next

Never settle for less

I feel that I'm going to mourn if I have to say that's it

You compliment my positive emotion

I once was so heartless down right selfish

But I share stuff with you I just can't help it

Give me your stable, share your thoughts

I trade you my freedom in exchange for your love

I summon the courage and I pray to above

I've been fighting so hard, take off my gloves

Undo my wraps, cover me in trust

You're the best contender so if I show you these words

My love and heart I surrender!

Chance meetings

Caught in a deadlock

Pretending we were lip locked

A strange kind of meeting

Eye to eye

Hands stretched out

Will you be mine?

Give me your heart and give me your mind

Can I be your lover if you give me a little time?

Slow-motion

My life lessons, the images perceived

Maybe hoping for an impossible blessing

I tried to play this hard ass game called love

I've strained and trained to maintain

Maybe it's in me

Maybe I'm the one to blame

Everything that makes you smile, may not be worth wild

Too persistent, maybe I should give up

Not to be held in esteem

Not be heard nor seen

Fade away right beyond your sight

Hollow to the core, I've done my part plus many more

Do I deserve to get this or maybe nothing more?

I just wish everyday was rain

Wash away the pain and these raw emotions that are

being slain

Cloudy days reclaim the bright lights of lovers who escape

my name

Now I'm trying to maintain

Show all parts that make me, me

But a donkey that's all you see

Sometimes, starting something new is all I see

Blinded to the reality love may not want me

Treading on thin ice I came off too nice

Used, abused, treated like a fool

I'm worthless in the eyes of the past

Beyond sound and wave lengths

End this frame of lies

Omit the negativity in my heart

Yet, the guilt only remains

If I slowed down time to show you how precious time is

Rewind things, relive them once more

Not rushing things, cheating on space and time

You think I'm too fast, promoting a sense of being forced

I'm surrounded by problems

Swallowed up in games

Sealed into shadows

Pride is being broken

No love in my eyes

As emotionless tears fall from my uncaring eyes

I do apologize; my heart could not come unbroken

It'll fix under pressure

Mend when I know you

I'm sorry, I want to love you

Press rewind

Make things screwed

Show me your love and I'll show you mine

Show me confidence, I'll unleash my potential

We'll heal in slow motion

Angel

I'm a sinner looking for a saint

Walking out in the open, head in the clouds

Nothing to be spoken

Dressed in all black, I'm mourning the void within my heart

Dressed in all black, I mourn the lack of happiness

Pieces Of My Heart: Wesley Anderson

Head held tall walking throughout the crowd

The wind begins the blow, symbols of the approaching winter season

Bringing about my lows and lack of energy

Summer is my main element

Fall is here now, and for a change I just want to fall

The coolness brings chills to my spine

My hands are freezing, but my heart beats hot as a furnace

Passing by people everyone becomes one big collage

Nothing life changing today, I say

Just an ordinary day

Out of nowhere like a ray of light

Out of nowhere like a god sent from heaven

A shimmering image appears

Made in his likeness in every way possible

Not at all perfect, but in my eyes it is perfect the way I see fit

The glow of your skin, it takes the frigid air away

Blinking over and over to make sure it's not an illusion

Pieces Of My Heart: Wesley Anderson

To prove in fact this dream is real

I see the sun reflecting off your eyes

This light must be hope

I feel it in my soul

It's a wish come true

Your smile resembles the shine of the gates of paradise

Decked in all white, piercing through my black and gloomy garments

There is the big dipper, there is the archer, look it's Orion

The stars, I can see them shine around your heart

My loneliness no longer near

The mourning, no longer hear

My smile is homing and is coming right after you

Every ill-fated entity needs a saving grace

With words unspoken you come to me and give a warm embrace

Much unexpected

You feel me, the same way I feel you

Its invisible, but I believe there are wings on your back

Pieces Of My Heart: Wesley Anderson

You give me this strange energy

Love, hope, and dreams orgasm into one

Intertwined like the sweet look of a candy cane

Spiraled together, the taste of nectar I want to savor

Running of my lips like an endless blue water river

Your kiss, forever embedded in my head

I know what you are

I believe in you

My sixth sense sees being the physical sense

You an angel

The skies they open wide

I see it in your eyes, you're an angel

The definition of a lover

I want to capture your essence

Extract the energy known as truth

Make my own existence a part of your world

Allow my selfish gain to no long remain

As I hold your embrace, lay you on my chest

Listen to the beat of my heart race

Two unrhythmic beats bound as a single tone

In my eyes I've seen through foolish lies, as I tossed those deemed unworthy aside

You're the only one, where my glory resides

Like an earthquake, you collapse my ground

Pin me down and reclaim what's yours

I exclaim and without shame I declare my lovers name

That makes me the sky, sailing away on winds of ambition

I want you for you and that's my sole mission

Pieces Of My Heart: Wesley Anderson

Give me your absolute truth, like my favorite liquor I'll down you

Take all you got like a quick shot

All fragments of the past, let's make it wash away

A clean slate today, let me show how it's meant to be

Eventually in time I'll make you mines

Not caught up on physical looks I want you for your mind

Let someone stand up who has a spine

If you say yes, then I have to soldier up, protect my line

Use my valor and guts to show you I can motivate me and you as "us"

Other relationships have just been depravation, a lack of sleep

Be my inspiration, control my restoration

Take me to place my heart only knows, grab my soul by the hand

Don't be a statistic, take a stand, and prove to me I deserve to be your man

I'm not "just a friends" let my best begin

I want your love, I don't want to pretend

I can offer a lot; take a chance see what I got

Understand me as a man, feel frustration

Inspect the morals of me, close your eyes and see what I see

This not a game you see your emotions mean a lot to me

I'm confident and confidence is key

I don't want to sound like a beggar so hear my plea

Look past all physical aspects, penetrate through

See the inner me inside

I've been that guy for so long but I want to be that special man

If only I had a chance, to make our future whole

Show the world I can love again

Place you on my shoulder I'd be your support

Nice and curious I'd put in work

Tell me what I have to say for it to be that way

I'd get on my knees and say whatever I'd have to say word for word

Other Books By The Author:

The author Wesley Anderson is partnered and Published with Maximize Publishing Inc. out of the Bronx N.Y.

1. Pieces of My Heart

2. Soul Cleanse Vol. II (Co- Author)

www.ingramcontent.com/pod-product-compliance
Lightning Source LLC
Chambersburg PA
CBHW072200090426
42740CB00012B/2334